Chinese New Year

Series Editors, China Titles:
NIGEL CAMERON, SYLVIA FRASER-LU

Chinese New Year

PATRICIA BJAALAND WELCH

With photographs by Sha Ying and
drawings by Clinton Phillips

OXFORD
UNIVERSITY PRESS

OXFORD

Oxford University Press is a department of the University of Oxford.
It furthers the University's objective of excellence in research, scholarship,
and education by publishing worldwide in

Oxford New York

Athens Auckland Bangkok Bogotá Buenos Aires Calcutta
Cape Town Chennai Dar es Salaam Delhi Florence Hong Kong Istanbul
Karachi Kuala Lumpur Madrid Melbourne Mexico City Mumbai
Nairobi Paris São Paulo Singapore Taipei Tokyo Toronto Warsaw

with associated companies in Berlin Ibadan

Oxford is a registered trade mark of Oxford University Press

Published in the United States
by Oxford University Press Inc. New York

First published 1997
This impression (lowest digit)
3 5 7 9 10 8 6 4 2

British Library Cataloguing in Publication Data

available

Library of Congress Cataloguing-in-Publication Data
Welch, Patricia Bjaaland, date.
Chinese New Year / Patricia Bjaaland Welch.
p. cm. — (Images of Asia)
Includes bibliographical references and index.
ISBN 0-19-587730-6 (hc : alk. paper)
1. Chinese new year. 2. China — Social life and customs.
3. Calendar, Chinese. I. Title. II. Series.
GT4905. W46 1997
394.2'61—dc20   96-17971
CIP

Printed in Hong Kong
Published by Oxford University Press (China) Ltd
18th Floor Warwick House East, Taikoo Place, 979 King's Road,
Quarry Bay, Hong Kong

Contents

Acknowledgements

According to Chinese tradition, one first thanks one's parents, and then one's teachers. To this should be added colleagues, friends, and spouse.

The list of those whose help and generosity have made this volume possible begins at Boston University, where I first began my study of Chinese history and eventually became a lecturer in Chinese philosophy and religion. It includes my former colleague, Arthur Lederman, an accomplished Sinologist and teacher, and Liu Baisha and Harald Bøckman, who guided my struggle through the early years of learning Chinese and who eventually became my good friends and perpetual mentors. I am forever indebted to all those individuals and institutions who have shared their largesse and patient expertise with me.

My sincere thanks go out as well to my two talented colleagues at *Asia Business News*, Sha Ying and Clinton Phillips, whose work with camera and hand illustrate this text. And of course to my spouse, Mathew, who shares my love of Asia.

This book is for my two daughters, Sonja Michele and Kari Victoria. May you find something that gives your lives as much pleasure and richness as my study of Chinese history and culture has given me.

Patricia Bjaaland Welch (Wei Lixia)
Lunar New Year's Day 1996

Chinese New Year 1997 to 2009

7 February 1997   Year of the Ox
28 January 1998   Year of the Tiger
16 February 1999   Year of the Rabbit
5 February 2000   Year of the Dragon
24 January 2001   Year of the Snake
12 February 2002   Year of the Horse
1 February 2003   Year of the Sheep
22 January 2004   Year of the Monkey
9 February 2005   Year of the Rooster
29 January 2006   Year of the Dog
18 February 2007   Year of the Pig
7 February 2008   Year of the Rat
26 January 2009   Year of the Ox

1

The Chinese Calendar

THE ANCIENT SYMBOL of *yin* and *yang*—the cir-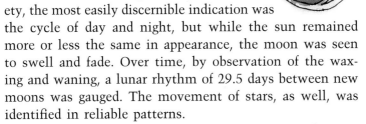
cle subdivided into two equal but asymmet-
rical halves by a sinewy line—says it all: life,
nature, this world as the Chinese have come
to know and understand it, is cyclical, a
continuous ebb and flow that repeats itself
as predictably as day follows night and
winter thaws into spring. To the ancient
Chinese observer living in an agrarian society, the most easily discernible indication was
the cycle of day and night, but while the sun remained
more or less the same in appearance, the moon was seen
to swell and fade. Over time, by observation of the wax-
ing and waning, a lunar rhythm of 29.5 days between new
moons was gauged. The movement of stars, as well, was
identified in reliable patterns.

With the invention of the first solar measure, the sun-
dial, came the discovery of the winter and summer sol-
stices and the autumn and spring equinoxes which together
extend over 365.25 days. The Chinese reconciled these
uneven solar and lunar cycles by adding an extra lunar
month at periodic intervals. Thus, the Chinese calendar
consists of repetitive cycles of 19 solar years, the whole
divided into 130 months of 30 days, 110 months of 29 days,
and 7 months of 'odds and ends'.[1]

The philosopher Confucius, who set the foundations for
much that traditional Chinese societies still hold dear today,
taught that order was the foundation of a stable society.
Order in the heavens meant order on earth (to such a degree

that climatic irregularities and unusual events were seen as portents of impending earthly chaos). Because the ability to foretell the coming seasons by astrological observations of the past was accorded such importance, China's astronomers rose to hold high offices in the imperial government. As keepers of the calendar and other records, one of their most solemn tasks was to predict and print each year's almanac. The almanacs and calendars themselves were held in such regard that they were accorded the highest honours: 'to issue a counterfeit or pirated edition was a penal offence, and falsification was punished by death' (Bredon and Mitrophanow, 1966: 5). Today, the giving of calendars and almanacs at the beginning of the new year is still a Chinese tradition.

The Chinese lunar calendar is divided into a cycle of sixty years, sometimes referred to as the Cycle of Cathay, consisting of five repetitions of each of twelve years. In Chinese culture each of these years is associated with an animal, displaying its own characteristics, and together they are known popularly through both East and West as the Chinese zodiac. The West has its counterpart in the solar signs, of which there are also twelve.

Chinese children are associated with the zodiac year in which they are born, and until modern times, when asked a chronological age, many would respond with the appropriate animal[2] rather than a precise year (*see* The Chinese Zodiac at the back of this book). The cycle begins with the year of the rat, continuing in the following order: ox, tiger, rabbit, dragon, snake, horse, sheep, monkey, rooster, dog, pig. It is a firm Chinese belief that destiny is the result of one's zodiac sign and, even today, horoscopes are often consulted before new pursuits, ranging from marriages to business ventures, are undertaken.

Careful examination of the traditional calendar, readily found throughout the Chinese world from Taipei office walls to Hong Kong taxi dashboards, reveals twenty-four 'special days' on the first and fifteenth days of each lunar month. In Chinese, these are known as the 'joints and breaths of the year' (*jieqi*), and identify the climatic, agricultural, and astronomical landmarks that comprise the calendar year. The first such date after the New Year, for example, is Lichun (The Beginning of Spring). Fifteen days later falls Yushui (Rainwater), marking the melting of the winter snow and the beginning of the spring rains.

Tradition dictated the activities to be carried out on each of these cosmic special days—garlic, for example, was to be dug up on Xiazhi (Arrival of Summer), which coincided with the summer solstice—and those Chinese holidays that generally, but not always, coincided with them. Today's Chinese New Year is a mélange of remnants from a number of ancient Chinese practices and holidays, including the winter solstice, an ancient exorcism festival, the lunar or official New Year, and Lichun (Bodde, 1975).

Much of the traditional Chinese world has been lost forever. In present-day Taipei or Hong Kong you are far more likely to see a Mercedes than a rickshaw. Today's successful Chinese 'gentleman' carries in his hand not a carved-gourd cricket cage but a cellular telephone. But there is one area of exception: tradition still dictates the practices and obligations of most Chinese holidays, and especially the most joyous and anticipated holiday of all, the Spring Festival or Chinese Lunar New Year. It is impossible, experts say, to overestimate its importance in the Chinese world.

2

Prelude: The Bitter Moon and Little New Year

THE CHINESE LUNAR YEAR begins on the first new moon after the sun enters Aquarius, which occurs between 21 January and 19 February of the Western calendar. It concludes on the fifteenth day of the first lunar month with the first day of spring, Lichun, which is also celebrated as the Lantern Festival.

The lunar month prior to New Year's Eve is crucial to the proper celebration itself, as it sets the framework for the ensuing holiday. Known colloquially as Hanlengyue, the Bitter Moon, because it contained some of the coldest weeks of the year, today it is more commonly referred to as Xiaoguonian (Little New Year), although this term should properly be reserved for the few days directly preceding New Year's Day. This period of saying goodbye to the past and preparing for the future consists of nearly a full month of activities.

The Eighth Day of the Twelfth Month: Remembering La

On the eighth day of the month prior to New Year a special porridge called *labazhou* is prepared. This 'soup of the eighth day'[3] resembles a thick gruel and is made from an assortment of grains or rice topped with nuts and dried fruits.[4] The actual recipe varies from province to province, but it is generally saltier in the north and sweeter in the south.

2.1 This small home shrine is used to worship household gods.

The origin of eating *labazhou* dates back approximately two thousand years to an ancient festival, called La, that occurred shortly after the winter solstice (Bodde, 1975: 49 ff.).[5] In olden times the porridge was prepared by the women of a household at first light, and the first bowl was offered to the family's ancestors, with others dedicated to the deities believed resident in every household (as at a gate, well, or door)(Fig. 2.1). Every member of the family was then served a bowl, with leftovers distributed to relatives and friends.

While La is generally understood to have been a religious, 'sacrificial' observance, its full significance is still unclear. The most common understanding of the practice was that it provided 'sustenance for [both] divinities and the spirits of the departed during the cold and darkness of winter' (Bodde, 1975: 55). Both the emperor and wealthy families distributed the rich porridge as a special gesture of favouritism.

No cooking is allowed during the early days of the new year and so, as the final month of the old year progresses, additional special dishes are prepared[6] and brought in for the new year. Once, pork and other meats were cured (a process called *la*, using the same Chinese character as that for the festival of the same name) and then dried, vegetables pickled, and duck eggs preserved. Sausages, smoked duck, and sweetmeats had to be purchased. All these activities took time. Their modern counterpart, of course, is standing in line in speciality shops (Plate 1), even those charging two to three times the normal price if their wares merit the New Year surcharge. Today, Chinese newspapers warn consumers to stock up before the season begins and to beware of fakes (for example, inexpensive shellfish peddled as the *de rigueur* abalone).

Cheo Kim Ban, of the Malaysian Chinese community, writes that the Straits Chinese (sometimes referred to as Peranakans or Babas, descendants primarily of Hokkien Chinese from Fujian province who settled on the Malay Peninsula and in its environs three to four hundred years ago),[7] made a great number of special cakes prior to the new year, 'most of which represented some good wish to sweeten human existence' (Cheo and Speeden, 1988: 48). The making of these cakes was fraught with superstition:

One of the most important cakes offered for welcoming the new year is still the sticky, steamed *kueh bakul*, or what the Chinese call *ni kueh*. It represents wholeness, good luck, riches and all that will be sweet in the coming year. [It] is made with great difficulty.... Many families are so scared of all the possible pitfalls in its making that they prefer to buy the cakes. Families in mourning do not make this cake; it is the custom for their relatives and friends to give them some. That is why you should not send this cake to friends for it implies that they are bereaved (Cheo and Speeden, 1988: 50–1).

Preparing the food for New Year takes several weeks and nearly every family member, with the exception of the adult males, lends a helping hand. One Hong Kong writer reminisced, 'I can remember the fun of helping to make rice cookies as a child. We would sit around a low table, filling wooden moulds with a rice flour mixture and pounding it in firmly with hammers to make "hard cookies". Often the pounding would get out of hand, especially when done by zealous teenagers, with the result that the cookies would be too hard to eat. Working together in this way and anticipating the feast a few weeks away created a special feeling of family closeness and unity' (Kong, 1989: 133–4).

The cookies described above are traditional New Year biscuits known in Mandarin as *chaomibing* (in Cantonese, *chaumaibeng*). The biscuits, relatively expensive and time-consuming to make, are generally round in shape and are decorated on top with auspicious characters and motifs. The old wooden moulds for forming the cookies can still be found in junk shops and at street fairs. As reported in a mid-1960s account of Hong Kong, the following mottoes were found on biscuits in a New Territories village:

Peace; Long life; Wealth; Peace for mankind; May wealth multiply; May sons and wealth be ours; Peace for old and young; Harmony and prosperity; World peace; May wealth increase daily; Harmony for 1000 years; Tranquillity; Foundation of wealth; Heaven helps a good man (Baker, 1979: 142).

Today's New Year biscuits are more commonly packaged in advance, but they still come in the traditional shapes with many of the same good-luck mottoes and designs (Plate 2).

The Twentieth Day of the Bitter Moon: Sweeping Out the Old

The night preceding the ancient festival of La was once known for the ceremony of the Great Exorcism, at which ornate rites were performed to eliminate evil, demons, pestilence, droughts, and poverty. These rites continued, in one form or another, both private and public, throughout Chinese history, the aim being 'to chase away the evil influences of a year that was drawing to its close and the virtues of which were entirely exhausted' (Gernet, 1962: 187).

During the Han dynasty (206 BC–AD 222), and with slight modification in the later Sui (AD 581–618) and Tang (AD 618–907) dynasties, the ritual performed on this night in the imperial court required 120 young eunuchs, ages 10 to 12 years, wearing red head-cloths and black tunics and carrying drums, to enact a drama symbolizing the suppression of all evils, led by an exorcist clad in a bear skin.[8] Amulets, bows, and arrows made of peachwood (believed to have apotropaic powers) were worn and carried, and reed brooms were borne by shamans and shamanesses.

Today, the most common ritualistic expression of the pre-New Year exorcism of old and malevolent forces, although far less colourful than formerly was the case in the imperial court, is still a major physical as well as symbolic undertaking: the spring house cleaning. The most modern, time-pressed, two-income family will want a thorough spring-clean, sometimes contracting with a professional house-cleaning service to achieve it. Decorators and paper-hangers do a year-end rush of business prior to Chinese New Year, accommodating those who can afford the luxury of new draperies, chair covers, cushions, and wallpaper. Even such items as footwear and towels, bedlinen and brooms are to be thrown out or replaced if possible.

Cheo, in his memoirs of his upbringing in a Malaysian Chinese household, writes of coming home from school one day before the New Year, 'sweaty and tired, and before I could take off my shoes, I would have spied the heavy brass candlesticks my mother had already lined up in the air-well. There was no need to tell us what to do. After lunch, we boys would set to rubbing, using up the polish lavishly, until our elbows ached. Another of our tasks was to clean the ornate carvings of the altar tables and blackwood chairs'. His sisters and aunts, he relates, were busy sewing new clothes and cushion covers and cleaning the ceiling. 'The ceiling, especially, had to be cleaned with bamboo fronds, to prepare for the coming of the New Year. The bamboo leaves are believed to sweep away any bad luck' (Cheo and Speeden, 1988: 48).

Settling of Debts and New Year Bonuses

Debts are also to be settled at the end of the old year. Generally, Chinese believe that all debts should be settled at three times of the year: at the first day of the first moon (the Lunar New Year), the fifth day of the fifth moon (the Dragon Boat Festival), and the fifteenth day of the eighth moon (the Harvest Moon or Mid-Autumn Festival). Modern debtors no longer follow these old dictates, but many will try to settle their household and credit card accounts by New Year's Eve. To begin the new year in debt is a bad omen for the future in any culture.

Luckily, there is the age-old Chinese custom of the New Year bonus. This sum almost always equates to at least one month's wages (giving it the common name of 'thirteenth-month bonus'), although it has become entangled with the idea of an 'annual bonus' in some firms so that the amount may differ depending upon each individual's employment contract and the profitability of the company. To give less than a month's wages, however, would be considered 'mean', unless the employment contract carefully spells out the figure in advance. The bonus is supposed to enable one to liquidate debts, purchase the necessary new outfits and accessories the new year demands, and 'provide at least one brief period of feasts, with plenty of those two prime luxuries, wine and pork' (Crow, 1938: 171). Nowadays in Hong Kong and Singapore it is also conveniently paid out just prior to the issuance of income tax assessments.

A side-effect of the New Year bonus has been employees' reluctance to change jobs until receipt of a bonus from their current employer. As a result, classified personnel ads are usually at a minimum before Chinese New Year, as employer and employee alike recognize the huge incentive for the employee to remain in place. The month following Chinese New Year is an entirely different story, however, and Chinese firms employing a large number of junior staff can experience as much as a 30 per cent staff turnover. Moral debts are also to be repaid before the arrival of the new year, with quarrelling parties reconciled, which explains why businesses selling felicitous greeting cards and New

Year gift baskets do a brisk business in this season.

For families with more restricted means, the Lunar New Year may be the only time of year when the members of the family sample a few luxuries of life. Lillian Ng, in a nostalgic novel telling of her growing up in China in the 1920s and 1930s, recalls, 'Chinese New Year [was] the only time Papa went to shop for cloth for sewing our suits and shoes, and for dried provisions such as sausages, smoked duck and sweetmeats for the New Year Feast' (Ng, 1994: 5).

Sending Off the Household Gods

In years past, on the twenty-third day (in the north) or twenty-fourth day (in the south)[9] of the month preceding New Year, a picture (or a simple piece of paper inscribed with the name) representing Zaowangye,[10] the Kitchen God, was propitiated with offerings of sweets and sent off to heaven via the kitchen stove to report on the family's behaviour for the year past. Frequently, the god's lips were smeared with honey, not so much to sweeten them as to keep them sealed,[11] and some families were said to inebriate the god by smearing opium on his lips or soaking his picture in wine to further ensure a good report (Bredon and Mitrophanow, 1966: 77).

Once upon a time, Zaowangye's benign countenance, dressed in judicial robes and headgear, was found in all Chinese kitchens. He is one of the oldest remnants of Chinese folk religion, associated with both fire and the hearth (the Chinese character *zao*, meaning 'stove' or 'oven', is composed of two parts: the radical on the left meaning 'fire', and on the right, 'earth'). In the past, incense was burned in his honour at every full and new moon.

Today, worship of the Kitchen God is officially 'forbidden' in the People's Republic of China (PRC), as he represents one of the Four Olds (customs, culture, habits, and ideas) that modern Marxist societies find awkward. Nevertheless, although little more than a symbolic nod in this age of gas stoves, microwave ovens, and electric rice cookers,[12] his paper portrait or name is still occasionally found in a Chinese kitchen. He is sometimes pictured holding a tablet on which he takes note of family events or with his wife by his side, a flock of children at their feet.

Because the interval between the twenty-third day and New Year's Eve is 'without gods' (who are known to be very demanding and easily displeased), it is a particularly advantageous time for human celebrations. Weddings held during this period are called 'weddings at the time of the year without the law' (Hong Kong China Tourism Press, 1993: 44) and are especially popular in the PRC: the proximity of the two festivities helps to stretch budgets and to aggrandize each celebration.

With the departure of the Kitchen God, Little New Year begins in earnest. In most Chinese communities, the opening of the season is signalled by the arrival of the local New Year market.

Auspicious Fruits and Decorative Plants

If you should visit Hong Kong prior to Chinese New Year and should take a tour of the New Territories, one of the

sights you will see is row after row of
budding saplings being cultivated for the
coming holiday: 'The farmers are trying to
bring them all to the point of imminent
bloom for New Year's Eve. The amount
of blossom that opens in the house during
the New Year celebrations determines the
wealth the household is to acquire during the coming year,
so careful timing is absolutely essential' (Baker, 1979: 16).

These force-grown saplings end up in the Chinese world's
special seasonal flower stalls and fairs that open from the
evening of the twenty-sixth day of the preceding month
through New Year's Eve. Famous Lunar New Year flower
markets are held on Hong Kong Island in Victoria Park and
in the New Territories at Shatin, Tai Po, and Yuen Long.
In Singapore, flower stalls form a part of the colourful lunar
market on Temple, Pagoda, and Mosque streets in Chinatown.
Even Bangkok's Chinatown has its flower stalls. While
some flower markets are open during the day, the best time
to pay a visit is always after sunset, when the markets
glow with the twinkling lights of hanging red lanterns.

In the past, certain plants were believed to ward off evil.
Arrows and amulets were fashioned from various *xianmu*
(spirit woods), such as plum, persimmon, pear, loquat, and
jujube, to be carried on one's person or displayed outside
dwellings to dispel evil spirits. Today, however, dwarf fruit
trees and spring bulbs such as the narcissus are valued
more for their symbolic and decorative than their supernatural
properties.

Peaches (*taozi*) symbolize immortality due to their affinity
with the famous peaches of immortality (*pantao*) that grow
in the garden of Xi Wangmu, the Western Queen Mother.
In Chinese art, Xi Wangmu is usually a stately and beautiful

2.2 The Chinese grapefruit, the pomelo (shown here piled on the centre table), is renowned for its curative and auspicious powers. Photo by Sha Ying.

Chinese woman who is often depicted with her two handmaidens, one of whom carries a tray of the famous fruit.[13]

Round yellow and orange-coloured fruit and vegetables such as oranges, melons, and pumpkins have long been associated with the moon by the Chinese and thus are also especially popular during this time of year. Mounds of oranges and pumpkins are an integral as well as an ornamental element of the modern Lunar New Year market, to which may be added the grapefruit known as pomelo (Fig. 2.2), and pineapples in such southern climes as Singapore.

Oranges are strongly associated with good fortune by the Chinese due to their golden colour (Plate 3). The tiny oranges known in English as kumquats are particularly linked with New Year in southern China and derive their

14

name from the Cantonese *kam* (meaning 'gold') and *kwat* (meaning 'orange'). In Mandarin, kumquats are known as *jinju*, *jin* being 'gold' and *ju* 'oranges' or 'tangerines'. The Chinese character for orange is composed of two components: the part on the left (the radical) means 'plant' and the part on the right means 'auspicious', hence the orange is an 'auspicious plant'.

So lucky are oranges that they are given as symbolic gifts throughout the season. Custom dictates that one be given an even number, usually two or four, offered and received with both hands. The recipient should return a number equal to those received.

Never mind that fruits or kumquat plants are sometimes recycled in gift giving, as is often the case with the West's Christmas fruit cake, the golden colour of the oranges ensures that they bring good luck no matter how many rounds they have made. Oranges, however, are not to be eaten until the second day of the new year, the day when the emperor customarily distributed the fruit to favoured members of the court.

Citrus fruits in general are important in Chinese life and culture. In south-eastern China there are said to be 'ninety varieties of oranges... [and] the Cantonese orange, a small fruit with a sweet taste, is the species from which the well-known Seville orange is derived' (Kong, 1989: 159). Some households add water that has been used to boil the leaves of the orange and the rind of the pomelo to their bath water, as 'the oil of the fruit, with its attractive pungent scent, acts as a cleansing agent' (Kong, 1989: 159). This is considered especially propitious for New Year's Eve baths but was always considered efficacious. When fourteen-year-old Lillian Ng became a household servant to a wealthy family in Guangzhou in the 1930s, she was told, 'You must bathe with pomelo leaves to banish bad luck and step over a brazier of fire for purification, pray to the god of the hearth—the Kitchen God—to ward off bad demons, before you enter the House of Tang' (Ng, 1994: 62).

Narcissus, known in Chinese as *shuixian* (water fairies), and sometimes called by Westerners the Chinese sacred lily (*Narcissus tazetta* var. *orientalis*), are symbols of good fortune, prosperity, and the spring. They are forced for the season in special shallow ceramic dishes using only clean pebbles and clear water. According to Chinese aesthetics, the plants should be slightly curved, not straight, and should be grown singly or in small numbers, not *en masse* (Li, 1956: 49). Daffodils are also popular as symbols of the coming spring.

Because the Japanese apricot or plum[14] tree blossoms at the end of winter (Plate 4), it too is a symbol of the approach of spring. Soame Jenyns (1966: 161) writes that a particularly popular New Year's gift during the reign of the Kangxi Emperor (r. 1662–1722) was a vase with a crackle glaze depicting plum blossoms, this design representing the cracking of winter ice with the first signs of spring. A famous poet of the Tang dynasty was said to have ridden out on a donkey into the snow to seek spring's first plum blossoms, and this theme has become a familiar image for the search for poetic inspiration.

Other traditional plants used ornamentally at New Year include the camellia and evergreen, as well as an inedible bright yellow citron, *Citrus chirocarpus*, which, because it is said to resemble one of the more frequently depicted hand positions of the Enlightened One, is called Buddha's Hand (*foshou*). It gains further merit from the similarity in sound between the words *fo* ('Buddha') and *fu* ('happiness')(Chavannes, 1973: 21).

Potted plants are well-established gifts for business associates and friends at the New Year, but cut flowers are strictly taboo as they are believed to symbolize being 'cut down' in the prime of life. The most common flower arrangements for the New Year are that widely known as the Three Friends of the Cold Season—the Japanese apricot, the bamboo, and the pine—and a composition composed of auspicious flowers symbolizing good luck, prosperity, and good fortune: the narcissus, nandina, camellia, and *lingzhi* fungus. Modern New Year floral arrangements in temperate climates often include the pussy willow (to which small golden 'peaches' or other appropriate decorations are sometimes affixed)(Plate 5). In northern China, plastic flowers are used to decorate winter-locked homes and offices.

3

New Year's Eve Preparations and Observances

3.1 This Lunar New Year street stall specializes in paper-cuts. The character in the foreground is *fu* ('good luck'). Photo by Sha Ying.

THE APPEARANCE in paper and household goods shops of bright red New Year greeting cards, printed spring couplets, pastel-coloured paper-cuts, multicoloured patterned mobiles, and door-god prints (Fig. 3.1) corroborates the closeness of the impending holiday. Sending New Year greetings bearing auspicious phrases and hanging talismans of good luck and good fortune during the holidays are believed to both dispel evil and attract good luck for the new year.

In Mandarin, 'new year' is *xinnian* (*xin*, 'new', *nian*, 'year'). The traditional New Year greeting in Mandarin-speaking communities is *Gonghe xinxi*: 'Respectful (*gong*) congratulations (*he*) and blessings (*xi*) for the new (*xin*) [year]', or more colloquially, 'Best wishes for the New Year'. Southern Chinese and Cantonese-speaking communities favour the greeting *Gonghei fat choy* (also transliterated as *Kung hei fat choi*, and in Mandarin, *Gonghe facai*), which adds the wish, 'May you also get rich' (*fat choy*), more commonly translated into English as the more mild, 'Wishing you a happy and prosperous New Year'.

New Year Couplets, Prints, and Streamers

In olden times, the term *taofu* was used to refer to charms made of peachwood, which were fashioned and carried on one's person or displayed outside homes to dispel evil spirits at the time of the Lunar New Year. The peach was considered to be so potent that the bark, wood, and roots of the tree, as well as the kernel of the fruit itself, were all a part of the well-stocked Chinese apothecarist's inventory. The term has come to refer, however, to couplets, five or seven characters in length, that are mounted on either side of a doorway at Lunar New Year. They are often accompanied by a third strip of red paper mounted horizontally above the door and bearing a propitious phrase of four or five characters (Plate 6), usually a final comment on the couplet beneath it. During the Tang dynasty, four lines of five or seven characters per line became a favoured poetic form; a number of poems on subjects relating to the new year and the arrival of spring are found in this format.

The more modern term for spring couplets, *chun lian*, is a literal translation and so is devoid of superstitious roots. New Year couplets are printed on bright red paper (Plate 7), red being an auspicious colour to the Chinese (although if there has been a recent death in the family couplets may be printed on blue or yellow paper instead).[15]

Carol Stepanchuk and Charles Wong (1991: 12), among others, believe that the first new year couplet to decorate a doorway was written by the tenth-century emperor Meng Zhang:

The New Year brings in overflowing good fortune,
The great festival is named Everlasting Spring.

Research has shown, however, that use of couplets did not become widespread until the Ming dynasty (AD 1368–1644).

Traditionally, New Year couplets were in perfectly matched pairs of syntactically balanced characters. Writing antithetical couplets (*duizi*) is considered an art; recognizing and understanding them is the mark of an educated person. Their 'essence is thesis and antithesis—antithesis between different tones and different meanings, resemblance in the relations between the characters in one clause and those in another clause' (Smith, 1965: 48). New couplets are composed regularly, but the old familiar ones are the most popular (Fig. 3.2). Better-known couplets include the following:

Fengtiao yushun song jiu sui
Daji dali ying sin chun
Propitious weather [for the crops] sends off the departing year [harvest];
Great happiness and great profit greet the new year.

3.2 Graced by a pair of fish and oranges to symbolize a surplus of riches, these two four-character spring couplets decorated with cash translate, from right to left, as 'Respectful salutations, [may you] become wealthy' and '[When you] attract wealth, precious [goods] follow'. Photo by Sha Ying.

Yishou bi nanshan
Fu ru donghai
May your longevity equal that of the Southern Mountains;
May your happiness be as vast as the Eastern Sea.

Another couplet, recorded by the historian Tun Li-Chen (1987: 99) of the Qing dynasty (1644–1911), reads:

Yitong taiping, zhen fu gui
Jiutian zhunse, da wen chang
May there be a single universal peace, with true wealth and honour;
May the spring colours of the nine heavens appear in profuse elegance.

21

Kong (1989: 134) also records a popular couplet:

Moderate winds and regulated rain; prosperity for the nation
and satisfaction among people;
With the sound of firecrackers, we bid the old year goodbye,
while peach charms appear in ten thousand households
to herald in all that is new.

Many common New Year wishes do not take the form of these beautifully balanced couplets but instead express simple New Year greetings. The most common consist of four characters, such as the following:

Jinyu mangtang (May your wealth [gold and jade] come
to fill a hall)
Dazhan hongtu (May you realize your ambitions)
Yingchun jiefu (Greet the New Year and encounter happiness)
Jiqing youyu (May your happiness be without limit)
Wanshi ruyi (May all your wishes be fulfilled)
Zhubao pingan (May you hear [in a letter] that all is well)
Yiben wanli (A small investment brings ten-thousandfold profit)
Fushou shuangquan (May your happiness and longevity
both be complete)
Zhaocai jinbao (When wealth is acquired, precious objects
follow)

Couplets are even hung outside garages, barns, bicycle sheds, pigpens, latrines—anywhere there is a door—but must bear appropriate greetings. Miniature couplet posters exist for the special gods of the earth, hearth, and home, all with standardized phrases. One for the Kitchen God, for example, may read, 'Make a favourable report to Heaven; protect people's lives on earth.'

New Year prints, once quite popular but now somewhat uncommon, covered a wide variety of subjects. While most attempted to convey auspicious scenes and wishes, they also 'served an important educational function, many representing historical or literary figures and conveying aspects of history and culture that were not accessible to the masses in books, as most of them were illiterate' (Wang, 1996: 55). Common were scenes from such classic novels as *Dream of the Red Chamber*, depictions of the Four Beauties (four famous and beautiful Chinese women), and other culturally significant images.

Especially popular at this time of year, but found year-round, are traditional paper-cut door streamers, produced by the women of the house and hung above doors both to decorate and to charm. Window paper-cuts are very popular in northern China and probably even predate spring couplets (Plate 8). Today, they have gained a popularity that has made them an independent folk art.

Good Luck Omens and Motifs

One of the most popular decorations found both on greeting cards and in New Year decorations are simple words such as *chun* (spring) and *fu* (good fortune), hung on walls or single doors (Plate 9). *Fu* is even more auspicious when hung upside down, as the Chinese word for 'upside down' (*dao*) also means 'to arrive' (Fig. 3.3). Hence, in Chinese, an upside-down *fu* sounds like 'Good fortune will arrive'.

Similarly, *fu* means 'bat' (of the winged, nocturnal variety), in addition to 'good luck'. As a result, bats are

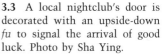

3.3 A local nightclub's door is decorated with an upside-down *fu* to signal the arrival of good luck. Photo by Sha Ying.

another popular Chinese New Year motif and are especially common paired with stylized coins to convey the hope that the good luck will be in the form of wealth.[16] Bats are such a popular symbol that they are found at all times of the year, decorating a multiplicity of articles from furniture to teacups.

Many New Year decorations depict money (perhaps in the belief that 'money attracts money'), often represented by ancient Chinese coins. Because in ancient China coins were commonly strung together for both safekeeping and storage, most had a hole in the centre. The most frequently depicted coinage is round (to represent heaven) with a square hole (to represent earth), a form once known as 'cash' (Plate 10). Now, of course, Chinese coins resemble other modern coinage, but to this day a pair of cash symbolizes wealth in Chinese countries. Another ancient form of money

1. Ablaze with red lanterns for luck, this Lunar New Year stall in Singapore features preserved meats. In the foreground can be seen a decorative pineapple (*onglai*), a symbol of good luck. In the background, a lion's head decorates a roof. Photo by Sha Ying.

2. An assortment of Chinese New Year cakes and cookies.

3. Due to their glowing golden colour, oranges are strongly associated with good fortune in the Chinese world. They are ceremoniously presented to family and friends during the New Year season to convey wishes for success and wealth. Photo by Sha Ying.

4. Plum blossoms, a symbol of spring's arrival, brighten a Chinese restaurant at the Lunar New Year.

5. A Lunar New Year flower stall is decorated with pussy willows from which lucky packets have been hung. Also visible is another favourite spring plant, plum blossoms. Photo by Sha Ying.

6. Spring couplets are the first sign of a new spring in an otherwise monotone grey Chinese courtyard. Photo by Sha Ying.

7. Stacks of spring couplets stand ready for customers in a Chinese New Year market.

8. This beautifully decorated window, displaying a variety of paper-cuts, was found in Shaanxi province. Photo by Sha Ying.

9. Auspicious New Year posters: the upper character reads *daji* ('great luck'), that in the middle, *chun* ('spring').

10. A typical New Year decoration with, from top to bottom, a gold ingot, a stylized Chinese coin (cash), and cascading firecrackers. The matching decorations on either side feature stylized bats (*fu*), which represent good fortune, surrounding a piece of jade, an auspicious mineral. An 'endless knot', a Buddhist symbol of longevity, completes the arrangement. To the far left can be seen a stylized gold ingot. Photo by Sha Ying.

11. These groupings of five oranges on sale in a local market will be presented as offerings at household shrines, temples, and ancestral halls during the holiday season.

12. This classic New Year arrangement contains pussy willows and plum blossoms, a Chinese grapefruit (pomelo), and a pineapple. The eight-sided sweet tray stands in front of a porcelain miniature tree bearing the magical peaches of immortality. Lucky oranges and kumquats, and in the background two firecrackers, complete this very auspicious arrangement. Photo by Sha Ying.

13. South-East Asia's version of the glutinous rice Chinese New Year cakes, *niangao*, wait for customers in a market. In northern areas, the cakes tend to be square or rectangular in shape.

14. In the doorway of a restaurant stands an arrangement of plum blossoms, firecrackers, red lanterns, and a beautifully calligraphed *fu* ('good luck'). Photo by Sha Ying.

15. A Chinese Lunar New Year market offers a variety of Chinese deities for sale together with whimsical plush rats for 1996, the Year of the Rat. The three deities are popularly known as Fulushou. From left to right, they are the Fu, God of Happiness; Lu, God of Prosperity; and Shou, the God of Longevity.

16. A scene from the annual fireworks display over Hong Kong harbour.

17. Two red lanterns decorate this courtyard during the Lantern Festival in northern China. Photo by Sha Ying.

18. Lights brighten the exterior of many Hong Kong hotels throughout the New Year season. Photo courtesy Omni Hongkong Hotel, Hong Kong.

that appears in New Year art resembles a curved dumpling but is actually an ancient form of silver and gold ingots.

Fish, particularly carp and perch, are repeatedly coupled with strings of coins and the dumpling-shaped ingots as the Chinese word for fish (*yu*) resembles that for abundance (*yu*), so fish have come to be a Chinese symbol of plenitude.[17] The coupling of fish and coins conveys the wish for an abundance of wealth.

A Chinese pun also gives us the more esoteric but well-known design commonly found on Chinese New Year cards of a goldfish (*jinyu*) wrapped (*bao*) in a lotus leaf (*he*). The meaning is 'an abundance of gold in your purse' (*hebao jinyu*), as *hebao* has the double meaning of 'a small purse', *jin*, 'gold', and *yu*, 'abundance'. Another popular traditional New Year print depicts a young child holding a goldfish and a lotus flower to convey the wish for 'wealth and harmony' (*he* meaning both 'lotus' and 'harmony')(Fig. 3.4).

A common New Year decoration shows a three-legged toad holding coins in its mouth to express the wish, 'May the New Year bring you riches' (if a small boy is also visible, the wish is for 'The double riches of wealth and sons'). According to Chinese legend, Liu Hai, one of the Eight Daoist Immortals,[18] once lured a poisonous toad into the open with a string of golden coins. Hence, toads are associated with greed and the acquisition of wealth. Because this is an ever-popular motif in Chinese imagery, the inclusion of a broom in a picture confirms its New Year use.

Due to the many meanings of the common Chinese sound *he*,[19] two brothers known as He He Er Xian (literally, 'two spirits named He') are also popular harbingers of good luck in the Chinese New Year. First of all, He is a common family name. Secondly, each of the He brothers holds a lotus (*he*) or a small box or bag (also *he)* which can be

3.4 This charming and popular print of a young child holding a giant goldfish and lotus is a classic New Year image.

interpreted as 'harmony' (*he*) and 'union' (*he*). These pudgy twins are generally depicted surrounded by such auspicious objects as flying bats and gold ingots, or together with Zao Shen, the God of Wealth. A painting or scroll of three boys playing together with a toad depicts the He twins together with Liu Hai. The plumper the boys, the greater the bounty.

Door gods

Pictures of the gate or door gods (*menshen*) that traditionally guard temples year-round are pasted on New Year's Day itself on both sides of residential entranceways to protect the buildings' inhabitants (Fig 3.5). Always sold in pairs, door-god posters are easily recognized by the figures' military

26

dress and weapons. Said to be quasi-historical, the original door gods have been linked to an ancient Daoist legend that tells of two brothers who lived under a giant peach tree, defending mankind by throwing all threatening spirits to hungry tigers (Bredon and Mitrophanow, 1966: 86).

The door gods have likewise been identified as two generals from the Tang dynasty who stood outside their sleepless emperor's tent one night to protect him from threatening devils so he could rest in peace. On the premise that 'If it works for the emperor, it'll work for me', the practice was quickly imitated in a more economical form by the masses. The white-faced general who proposed the scheme is known as Qin Shubao in Taiwan but is more commonly called Qin Qiong in mainland China. His dark-faced companion is known as Yuchi Jingde in Taiwan and Yuchi Gong on the mainland.

3.5 An ancestral hall in Hong Kong's New Territories, door gods painted on its tall portals. Photo by Nigel Cameron.

Although not depictions of a traditional door god, pictures and statues of another folk hero from the Tang dynasty are also popular New Year decorations. He is Zhongkui, also known as the Demon Chaser (*zhuogui*), and is regarded as a protector against demons and evil spirits throughout the year. The ferocious, heavily bewhiskered Zhongkui is usually portrayed balanced on one leg and waving a sword in the air. Occasionally, he wears a wreath of peach blossoms, and often he is depicted with a bat (for luck) either flying about or resting on his shoulder.

Zhongkui is also strongly associated with the Dragon Boat Festival. On this particularly dangerous day, the fifth day of the fifth month of the lunar calendar, Zhongkui is said to have drunk a magic elixir of poison (*wudu*) drawn from the 'five poisonous creatures'—the scorpion, toad, centipede, spider, and snake—and ascended into heaven.

New Year's Eve

On New Year's Eve, the preparatory chores completed and the doorways swept and watered, the family—freshly bathed, clad in new clothes, and with hair newly clipped and coiffed—gathers together to bid the old year farewell, offer filial prayers to ancestors, and welcome in the new year. As many generations as possible are expected to take part in the occasion, with family members sometimes travelling great distances to attend.

The importance of the traditional New Year gathering has given rise to one of the Chinese world's most horrific if short-lived problems, the pre- and post-holiday New Year traffic jam. For the forty-eight hours preceding New Year's Eve, every bus and train station, every airport in the Chinese world is jammed to the breaking-point with individuals trying to get home for the celebration. The border crossing between Hong Kong and the PRC sees hundreds of thousands of people each day in the days before New Year's Eve. Most are burdened with great mounds of gifts, ranging from dried ducks to boxes of candied sweets, electrical appliances to the latest laser discs.

During the early part of the evening, traditionally 9 to 11 pm, incense is lit on the ancestral altars. Prayers to bid farewell to the old year, led by the senior male of the household, are offered first to Heaven and Earth, then to the household gods and the family ancestors. The simplest offering consists of three sticks of incense (offerings are always in groupings of one, three, or five)(Plate 11). More commonly, especially at such an important holiday as the New Year, the offering will include oranges or tangerines and such symbolic fruit as mangoes, pears, and pineapples, together with tea and the three traditional meats: pork, with either fish and chicken, or duck and goose. The grandest offering consists of a whole roasted pig. Some Straits Chinese families would 'include the favourite brand of cigars or cigarettes of the male ancestors' among the New Year offerings (Cheo and Speeden, 1988: 52).

In olden times, doors were locked and sealed with red paper as the old year ended, so no hint of lingering bad or worn-out luck could steal its way back in to spoil the new year. Firecrackers were set off to scare any lingering bad spirits, and families sat up throughout the night (a practice known as *shousui*). Tun (1987: 101), recorder of Beijing's traditional festivals, tells of the one-time practice on New Year's Eve night of covering the courtyard with crunchy stalks 'to give warning of the approach of any [evil] spirits', a practice with which any Western child who has left a Christmas Eve floor lightly floured to catch Santa's footprints would surely sympathize.

Today firecrackers, once used to scare away evil spirits, now burst away in the streets of those few remaining Chinese communities where laws permit them. When the precise moment of the New Year arrives it is welcomed with incense and lights, before the household door is finally closed and locked for the night. It is not to be opened again before morning, when it is formally unsealed, often with the recital of a felicitous phrase. This used to be called 'opening the door of fortune' (*kaicaimen*). It was at this point in times past, but little seen today, that a second set of ceremonial prayers was offered to the gods of Heaven and Earth, the household deities, and ancestral spirits. In the morning, parents are honoured by being served the year's first cup of tea by their children, regardless of age (Bredon and Mitrophanow, 1966: 92ff).

In the distant past, the rituals of New Year's Eve took place outside, in the courtyard of the home. Modern apartment complexes have done away with the traditional Chinese home, so most ceremonies now take place in front of the family altar many families still maintain, no matter how small their dwelling or modern their residence.

4

The New Year: Attracting Good Luck

ONCE THE NEW YEAR arrives, for fear of chasing away good luck, no sweeping, dusting, or washing of the house is permitted until the end of the first day of the year. Traditionally, there was to be no chopping, nor use of sharp objects such as scissors, knives, or needles. In olden times, even wells were covered to prohibit the drawing of water (Bredon and Mitrophanow, 1966: 90).[20] No cooking was permitted until after the New Year, although this rule is neatly circumvented today, as it always has been, by the preparation in advance of as much food as possible.

Today, in the most traditional households no swearing, negative, or 'dangerous' phrases are to be uttered, even such words as 'tiger' or 'sick', lest they give rise to the actuality. Children are not to be scolded or punished. Hair is not to be washed lest good luck also be washed away. The number four (*si*) is not to be spoken, as it is a homophone for 'death'. No dishes are to be overturned or broken, although if something is broken a quick *Luo di kai hua* ('Flowers blossom from the ground') can repair the bad omen, according to one modern Singapore writer (Chen, 1996: 3). All are to be on their very best behaviour, since it is believed that every member plays a role in influencing the luck of the family in the new year.

Auspicious Food

'The Lunar New Year is a time when many things such as food—from humble peanuts to sweet Mandarin oranges—

31

4.1 Cans of abalone await New Year shoppers. Note the appropriate brand name, New Moon, on some of the cans.

are said to bring good luck to the recipient or eater' (Chen, 1996: 3). Every sound uttered, every morsel consumed during the early moments of the new year is imbued with a richness of symbolism far surpassing that imaginable in the West. The dining table is no exception, and especially the first meal of the new year, which often features nine (*jiu*) courses or dishes to rhyme with the word meaning 'forever' (also *jiu*).

Certain foods, because of their relationship to auspicious words of similar sound, are especially popular. Practices vary from province to province and dialect to dialect, but some well-known examples are dried seaweed (*cai*, which relates to 'prosperity' or 'wealth', as in *facai*, 'becoming rich'), oysters (*hao*, similar to 'good events', *haoshi*), and abalone (*baoyu*, similar to 'guaranteed excess', *baoyu*) (Fig. 4.1). Singapore families add pineapple (*onglai*) tarts to the list, as their name resembles 'the arrival of good luck' in Hokkien, the dialect of one of Singapore's oldest Chinese communities.

As mentioned earlier, fish is considered auspicious because the sound of its generic term (*yu*) is identical to that meaning 'surplus', 'abundance', and 'profit'. The opening of shellfish symbolizes the opening of new horizons. In Hong Kong, 'a family celebrates New Year's Eve with a dinner in which the first course served is a special two-fish dish. The fish (yu) are prepared so that they remain whole, from head to tail. However, they are not eaten but are placed by the family rice jar after dinner, so that the abundance (yu) they represent will carry over to the new year' (Kong, 1989: 153). A special fish dish, known as 'Prosperity Raw Fish', yusheng, traditionally served on the seventh day of the new year, is discussed in the appropriate section below.

Soups that contain dumplings shaped like gold and silver ingots guarantee prosperity to the Shanghainese. Beijing residents down meat-filled dumplings called jiaozi at midnight, as jiaozi 'sounds like a term that means the meeting of the last hour of the old year with the first hour of the new' (A Year of Good Fortune, 1993: 18), as well as 'procreate and have sons'. The shape of hard-boiled eggs symbolizes a happy reunion. Cellophane noodles are said to resemble silver chains. Fish and chicken are the most popular main courses, as yu is homophonous with 'abundance' and ji is a homophone shared by 'chicken' and one of the most common auspicious wishes for the new year, that of 'luck'.

Cantonese traditions result in the culinary inclusion of mushrooms, for longevity, as well as a stringy vegetable that looks like hair, as the words for 'hair vegetable' sound like a term for prosperity. Pig's feet represent 'being lucky in winning money in gambling', while the phrase for pig's tongue is a homonym for a saying that 'everything will go smoothly' (Ng, 1994: 121). The term for dried oysters (houxi) resembles 'good business', and shrimp (ha) sounds like 'happy laughter'.

If long noodles representing longevity are served, one never breaks them up in order to eat them more easily; this would be considered an ill omen symbolizing a life cut off before its prime. These noodles are often served at birthday parties, where the same etiquette demands that they be eaten unbroken.

All these traditional, auspicious dishes have the most delectable names: 'Mist of Harmony', 'Broth of Prosperity', 'Gold Cash Chicken', and so forth. There are even 'lucky' drinks for the season, *yuanbaocha*, whose name refers to the ancient Chinese gold or silver ingots called *yuanbao*, being the preferred 'lucky' tea (*cha*). Special regional dishes, such as cured sausages, barbecued pork, and smoked duck, complement each family table and add to the special-ness and extravagance of the feast. There is also a likely link between the popularity of cured (*la*) meats at this time of year and the ancient exorcism festival La, described above, in that they are not only homophones but share the same Chinese character.

Here is just one sample menu, this one advertised by Singapore's Harbour City restaurant during the New Year season 1996. The significance of each dish would not be lost on most Chinese celebrants.

Auspicious Spring New Year Menu
Prosperity Raw Fish Salad
Pig's Shank with Lotus Root Soup
Stewed Dried Oyster with Black Moss
Roasted Pullet Marinated with Minced Garlic Sauce
Steamed Sultan Fish with Minced Ginger
Braised E-Fu Noodles
Red Bean Cream with Glutinous Dumplings

After-dinner and between-meal sweets are sold in special partitioned eight-sided cardboard or lacquer containers (*henian quanhe*, where *henian* means 'to extend New Year greetings', and *quanhe* means 'all harmonious')(Plate 12). Groupings of eight are considered especially auspicious (in Cantonese, 'eight', *baat*, sounds like 'to prosper'). Each section's proffered delicacy has a double meaning based on its name or characteristics. Lotus seeds are one of the traditional eight components, because the word for lotus, *lian*, is a pun on the word meaning 'to repeat', so the lotus expresses the continuity of good fortune, be it in wealth, promotion, or descendants.

Other sought-after snacks are peanuts, red dates, pomegranate seeds, almonds, pears, candied tangerines, peaches, and apricots—all symbolizing good luck in one form or another. Because flowers, fruits, nuts, and seeds hold the powers of fertility and fecundity, the Chinese have linked them linguistically to the very concept of fertility through the character *zi* (Fig. 4.2). This has brought about an abundance of symbolic double meanings. For example, the sound *li*, which has many homonyms, can mean 'pear', but also 'a state of change'. When linked to the character *zi*, meaning 'seed', 'kernel', 'grain', and 'child', *lizi* means both 'a pear' and 'begetting children'. Lotus seeds (*lianzi*) have the double meaning of 'children, one after the other'.

Platters of auspicious seeds, nuts, and fruits are also known as *zaosheng guizi* or *liansheng guizi*, which sound, respectively, like phrases meaning 'to soon realize the birth of noble sons' and 'the continuous birth of noble sons' (*A Year of Good Fortune*, 1993: 19). And while peanuts are very auspicious (their name, *huasheng*, is homophonous with the classical Chinese Buddhist term for rebirth),[21] porridge, considered a poor man's food, is definitely not to be served or consumed lest it bode a poor future.

4.2 Nuts and seeds are especially important components of sweet trays during the Lunar New Year because of the double meaning of their generic name (*zi*), also a homonym for 'offspring'. Individual seeds and nuts have additional double meanings.

One classic Chinese New Year dessert is a sweet steamed rice pudding or cake (*gao*) made with glutinous rice flour, water, and sugar and known as *niangao* in Mandarin and *ninko* in Cantonese. In Singapore and other southern Chinese communities, every household will serve *niangao* at least once during the holiday season, because its consumption expresses the desire 'to rise [*gao* or *ko*] in rank or prosperity year after year' (*nian*). Great mounds of cellophane-wrapped *niangao* characterize every Chinese New Year market (Plate 13).

In South-East Asia, *niangao*, which requires approximately nine hours of steaming in a banana-leaf mould to attain its characteristic round shape and reddish-brown colour, is most often served sliced, steamed, and rolled in lightly salted grated coconut or dipped in a light batter before frying. In the north, *niangao* is more characteristically square or rectangular in shape. *Niangao* is often presented to business associates and friends as a special seasonal gift.

The making of *tsintui*, an especially popular Cantonese dessert of round sesame cakes, is linked to a rhyme that may be translated, 'As the sesame cakes are rolled, the house is filled with silver and gold.'

Red Packets: Hongbao, Laisee, *and* Angpow

At some point on New Year's Eve, after New Year greetings have been given and dinner consumed, children and unmarried members of the family will receive their first red packets of 'lucky money' (Fig. 4.3). These packets are known as *hongbao* in Mandarin, *laisee* in Cantonese, and *angpow* in Hokkien.

4.3 An offering of five oranges, symbolizing good luck, is arranged together with a selection of 'lucky money' packets. From right to left, there are three envelopes with variants of the character *fu*, an auspicious saying, a packet with a horse design from a Year of the Horse, a lion mask, a packet from a Year of the Dog, and a packet bearing the auspicious phrase, *Jixiang* ('lucky' or 'good omens').

The rules that govern the exchange of the little red envelopes, bearing New Year designs in gold and containing crisp new notes, are easy: adults give to young people, the married to the unmarried. The received sum must be an even number, preferably in the form of two bills or a combination of bills that add up to the 'lucky' numbers 8 or 88 (remember that 'eight' in Cantonese is a homonym for 'prosper'). In modern times, this translates into senior managers handing out envelopes to employees (patrons likewise give to such 'regulars' as doormen and hairdressers). 'Aunties' and 'uncles' give to their friends' children as well as to their own nieces and nephews. Moreover, 'if a person goes to a friend's home to visit during the days of the celebration of the New Year, and there is someone else visiting in the home who has children, even though he does not know them, he must also give lucky money... [or] people will say, "Oh, this person does not have lucky money," and this will bring bad luck to him' (Ng and Ingram, 1983: 90). Maids of visited families should also be given lucky money, which is usually discreetly placed under a plate or saucer as would be done with a restaurant tip.

The modern rules of *hongbao* were pragmatically summarized in a Singapore newspaper as follows: give 'depending on how close you are to the recipients or their family, or how much they have given to your children in the previous year's *hongbao*' (Chen, 1996: 3). And during New Year, never venture out-of-doors unprepared—without a small stack of packets in your pocket—as you never know who you will meet: 'Chinese people must always be prepared' (Ng and Ingram, 1983: 93).

Hongbao is presented to its recipient with a traditional three-dip bow, and good manners dictate that recipients not open the envelopes until out of sight of the giver. Since modern marketers have discovered that the decorative envelopes are just the right medium for sponsors' logos and greetings, most banks in communities with Chinese populations provide free *hongbao* packets when filling customers' requests for crisp new bills to fill them.

The First through Fourth Days

During the Chinese New Year season, visitors to Chinese countries who expect to see noisy, celebrating crowds are often surprised at the empty and quiet streets on the first day of the new year. 'The New Year sun rises on muted cities in China', wrote two Western observers early in the twentieth century (Bredon and Mitrophanow, 1966: 106). Very little stirs on the first two days of the year, for these are the days when the older members of the family stay at home, while the younger members pay New Year calls on close relatives, teachers, and, traditionally, employers and other potential benefactors, such as government officials.

The first day of the year focuses on the family, as no holiday more than the Lunar New Year reaffirms the importance of family and kinship in Chinese culture. The day is normally spent at home eating, drinking, and playing games, especially those that involve an element of luck and winning money. Everyone is dressed in new clothes, red being a favourite colour of the season, and women wear their best jewellery and accessories.

Until very recently, Chinese families would consume vegetarian meals on New Year's Day out of respect for the Buddha's prohibition against taking life and from the desire to avoid such ill-omened acts on the first day of the year

4.4 Dried fish is a popular New Year dish both because of the double meaning of the word *yu* and because many Chinese do not eat meat on New Year's Day out of respect for the Buddha's prohibition against the taking of life.

(Fig. 4.4). Some still continue this custom, but for many it has become a practice devoid of religious meaning, much as many modern-day European Christians still serve fish as the main meal on Christmas Day. When a team of sociologists conducting research in a small Hakka hamlet in Hong Kong's New Territories asked the meaning of this traditional custom, one of the villagers replied, 'There is no special meaning. Since we eat only meat dishes on New Year's Eve, we eat more vegetables on New Year's Day' (Berkowitz and Brandauer, 1969: 48).

The Second Day: Kainian

The second day of the new year is known as the *kainian*, 'beginning of the year', and is spent at home or visiting relatives and friends. A large lunch looms on most families' agenda. Visiting friends during Chinese New Year is such an expected and common practice that a Malaysian author wishing to emphasize the unusualness of a character wrote, 'I doubt if anyone who knew Meng in school ever visited him at home. He discouraged such visits almost aggressively, even at the Lunar New Year' (John, 1991: 44).

Hostess gifts—steamed cakes, *niangao*, fruit, and boxes of candies and sweets—are always taken on New Year calls. Hostesses serve tea, together with sweets, preserved fruits and nuts, and some a special boiled dumpling known as *bobo*, which is made of white flour with special fillings (sometimes including pieces of gold or silver or precious stones, much as English plum puddings served at Christmas used to contain small charms) to augur the future.

Decorating many homes are artificial money trees, constructed formerly from large pine and cypress branches but today more commonly from pussy willows or plum-tree branches stuck into vases and decorated with coins, red packets, and other good luck symbols. These are also popular decorations in office buildings, restaurants, and hotel lobbies, which often add artificial strings of bright red 'firecrackers' to liven up the display (Plate 14). Stylized money trees made from glass and plastic are one of the items found in most Lunar New Year markets, as are paintings and statues of popular Chinese folk heroes and deities (Plate 15).

In olden times, the second day of the year was also celebrated as the God of Wealth's birthday, and it was understood that he would visit your family if you were one of the fortunate ones. As a result, old pictures of the god were taken down to be replaced by new ones (traditionally placed on the wall facing the door of the house). 'Beggars and other unemployed people circulate[d] from family to family, carrying a picture [of the God of Wealth and] shouting, "Zao Shen dao" (The God of Wealth has come!)' (Kong, 1989: 48). On hearing such good news, the head of a household would usually open the door and, of course, reward the messengers with 'lucky money'. In more recent times, children have joined the bandwagon to add to their *laisee* largesse.

This date also coincides with Hong Kong's famous annual New Year fireworks display (Plate 16). One of Hong Kong's most magnificent sights, the fireworks (bearing such suitably picturesque names as 'Basket of Flowers in the Spring') are launched from barges in the harbour to the accompaniment of a thundering orchestral background broadcast throughout the Territory. Corporations pick up the tab for the popular government-organized event, which in 1996 cost US$600,000. Six tons of fireworks were set off during the 25-minute display.

The Third and Fourth Days

The third day of the new year was traditionally spent avoiding one's relatives, as superstition warned that visits on this day could result in quarrels. Hakka villagers in rural Hong Kong in the 1960s called it the Day of the Poor Devil and believed everyone should stay at home (Berkowitz and Brandauer, 1969: 49). For many families it is a day of rest, while others venture out to traditional theatricals, lion or folk dances, or (today) to the cinema. This is also traditionally the date of one of Hong Kong's largest horse-races, held at the Shatin race-course in the New Territories.

The third day is another auspicious date to visit the temple of the God of Wealth, in particular to plead for 'inside' support at the racetrack, mah-jong table, and Stock Exchange. In major Chinese cities, such as Taipei and Hong Kong,[22] traffic police need to be called in to cordon off roads surrounding the most popular temples.

At the temples, once the requisite incense has been lit and offerings made, the serious task begins: having one's fortune told. A popular means of divination, known as *qiu qian* (in Cantonese, *kauh chim*), entails the rhythmic shaking of a bamboo tube filled with numbered sticks until a single stick falls out. The number is noted, and for a small 'donation' the petitioner is given a slip of paper or a reading corresponding to the divined number.

On the fourth day of the new year, the focus is on business. Corporate 'spring dinners' kick off, and most restaurants will be busy with such bookings for weeks. Traditionally, the fourth day was when employees were sacked, firing someone before the New Year (and their reception of the thirteenth-month bonus) being considered unnaturally cruel.

Lion Dances

Lion dances are usually the domain of 'athletic associations', trained amateur troupes of young men who, working in pairs and sharing a large, colourful, and shaggy papier mâché lion costume (one person controlling the head and the other the hindquarters), dance to the accompaniment of thunderous cymbals, gongs, and drums. Because lions were believed to have power over the earth, such dances were originally held in rural villages to ensure successful harvests, particularly during the period immediately after the

4.5 At this lion dance, being performed outside a small shop, a packet of 'lucky money' has been hidden in the sprig of kumquats on the ground at the dancers' feet. Photo by Sha Ying.

New Year and culminating in the Lantern Festival. In Cantonese, 'dancing lions' (*mosi*) is homophonous with 'no trouble', but no such pun works in Mandarin.

The most common contemporary New Year's lion dance has less to do with fertility than with wealth (Fig. 4.5). In the dance known as *caiqing*, a lion chases a red *hongbao* packet symbolizing wealth (*cai*), usually held aloft by a young boy whose main job is to tease the lion. There are a number of variants: sometimes the red packet is hidden in a head of green lettuce, lettuce (*shengcai*) being homophonous with 'life riches' (*sheng*, 'life', *cai*, 'riches'). Ng (1994: 3) describes a typical New Year's lion dance which took place in the Dixon Street Mall in Sydney, Australia, in 1992: 'from the shop awnings dangle green lettuces tied with red-packet good luck money for the dancing lion to retrieve'.[23] Another popular lion dance features a third dancer wearing the mask of a laughing Buddha and holding a banana-leaf fan.

Today, lion dances are enjoying a renaissance in some areas and seeing a decline in others. In Singapore, the number of lion dance troupes, bearing such names as the Singapore Dragon and Lion Athletic Association, has doubled in the past ten years. Lion dances are also performed at weddings, significant birthdays, launches of new business endeavours, and hotel openings (Fig. 4.6). Many purists lament that, unfortunately, the traditional steps and gestures are being supplanted by new, more athletic and contemporaneous acrobatic stunts.

4.6 The manager of the New World Hotel paints in the lion's eyes at the beginning of a traditional lion dance outside this popular Kowloon hotel. According to a popular legend, representations of animals can 'come alive' when the final touch of the drawing of the eyes is complete. Photo courtesy New World Hotel, Hong Kong.

The Fifth Day: 'Breaking the Five'

All the taboos of the New Year period formally end on the fifth day. Formerly, when one wasn't allowed to cook rice until the fifth and last day of the five-day New Year celebration, this day was known as *Powu* (Breaking the Five). Today, few Chinese communities enjoy the luxury of a five-day holiday, and most people are back to work on the fourth day.

Also known in some communities as the Day of the God of Wealth (or Birthday of the God of Wealth), this is another auspicious day to visit temples. In some parts of China a picture of the God of Wealth is burned on the sixth day, sending him off until the next year. Traditionally, all New Year gambling was to end until resumed the following year (not that gambling ever truly ceases in any Chinese society).

Day Seven: The Universal Birthday of Human Beings

Chinese folklore designates the first eight to ten days of the new year as the birthdays of animals and grains: the first day, chickens; the second, dogs; the third, pigs; the fourth, sheep; the fifth, oxen; the sixth, horses; the seventh, human beings; the eighth, grains; the ninth, fruits and vegetables; and the tenth, stone. As a result, each day has had a special activity, belief, or superstition associated with it, and if any of the these 'first' days was overcast it was believed to bode ill for the animals or objects associated with it.

On the seventh day of the New Year, considered the birthday of all humans (renri), it was thought best to stay at home and to consume red beans (seven for men, fourteen for women) as protection against sickness in the year to come.[24] This was traditionally the day when everyone added a year to their age (the recognition of individual birth dates considered egocentric and therefore unimportant to the ancient Chinese), and it is still marked in some regions by the exchange of tinfoil cut-outs, in the shapes of human or other figures, and celebratory dinners. Fireworks are also sometimes seen on this day, as it is also the birthday of the God of Fire (Hong Kong China Tourism Press, 1993:

51). Known variously as Nanfang Chidi, Nanfang Jun, Hui Lu, and Huo Shen, he is commonly depicted with a red face, a third eye located in the middle of his forehead, and carrying a wheel or ball of fire.

Southern Chinese mark the day by consuming *yusheng*, a traditional Cantonese and Teochew[25] dish made of fish and vegetables.[26] Its name has the literal meaning of 'live fish' or 'raw fish', but it has the added meaning of 'an abundance of life' (*yu*, 'abundance', *sheng*, 'life'). *Yusheng* is eaten at least once during the season to ensure longevity and prosperity. Similar to a salad, *yusheng* has to be tossed, which has given rise to the familiar shared toast of 'Lo hei!', said before everyone gets into the action of mixing the dish. 'Lo hei!' is best translated as 'Pushing forward everyone's good luck'. 'Lo Hei with us!' shout newspaper ads throughout the region. Once a novelty, *yusheng* has become very popular and is now served throughout the New Year season. As a result, the import of raw fish to sustain this tradition has become a million-dollar business in South-East Asia.

The Ninth Day: Birthday of the Jade Emperor

The Jade Emperor, Yuhuangdi, is a Daoist god, the supreme deity of the pantheon to whom the Kitchen God and other lesser gods report at the end of each year. In the Baba, Hokkien, and Teochew communities, the god is known as Ti Kong Seh. Far less popular and not related to the preceding seasonal holidays, his birthday is nevertheless sometimes observed at local temples. Some communities celebrate his birthday on the eve, others on the morning of the ninth day of the new year. Straits Chinese family and communal altars are draped in special embroidered cloths on the Jade Emperor's birthday, and sugar-cane stalks, once symbolizing abundant harvests, are set alongside each end to express the desire for plenitude in the year to come.

The Tenth Day: Rats' Wedding Day

On the tenth day of the New Year, agricultural Chinese communities avoid implements made of stone in order to honour them on their day. In some regions, this day is also celebrated as the Wedding Day of Rats, but the date varies and the nuptials are also celebrated on the twelfth, seventeenth, or twenty-fourth by the sprinkling of grain or other foodstuffs as a contribution to the rodents' 'wedding feast'.

5

The Lantern Festival

THE FIFTEENTH DAY of the first lunar month, which corresponds to the first full moon of the new year, is celebrated as Dengjie, the Lantern Festival (Yuensie in Cantonese) (Plate 17), and marks the official first day of spring and the conclusion of Lunar New Year festivities. If the period immediately prior is devoted to sweeping out the old and scaring away potentially malevolent spirits, the period immediately after the arrival of the New Year focuses on welcoming the light, warmth, and promise of a fertile new time blessed by benevolent spirits.

Scholars believe that the Lantern Festival and its many observances may have started as an archaic festival (dating back as far as the Han dynasty) to mark the change-over from the darkest part of the year to the brilliance of spring (Tun 1987: 6). If so, it bears a marked resemblance to the ancient Roman Festival of Lights (celebrated with wintergreen boughs lit by small candles), which occurred around the winter solstice and which scholars believe came to be intimately involved with the celebration of the Christian Christmas.

It is thought that with the end of the New Year festivities the souls of one's ancestors returning to the nether world are best guided by the lights of their descendants' lanterns. Throughout China, however, there is also an interesting connection between lanterns and fertility that fits well with the symbolic arrival of the new year. It is recorded that in some communities in Yunnan province a lantern known as the 'Children and Grandchildren Lantern' is placed under the bridal bed. Elsewhere, 'a lantern was hung under the bed of pregnant women.... Women were said to like walking along under lanterns, in the belief that they would be fertile' (from the correlation of *deng*, 'lantern', with *ding*, 'an adult male liable for military service')(Eberhard, 1986: 159–60).

5.1 A procession during the Lantern Festival, late nineteenth century. Print courtesy Antiques of the Orient, Singapore.

During the Lantern Festival, the Chinese world diverts itself with theatrical performances, lion dances, and traditional foods, but the central focus is lanterns: grand and diminutive, round and multifaceted, their bright, glowing colours complementing their myriad shapes and designs (Fig. 5.1). Until the fall of the Chinese empire in 1911, wealthy families would vie with one another for the most spectacular lanterns, and the costs of lanterns made of transparent horn, lacquer, glass, silk gauze, and shell far surpassed the yearly earnings of the average Chinese worker. For 'three days and three nights', Jacques Gernet writes of a festival during the thirteenth century, 'the townspeople ruined themselves by the amount they spent on food and drink. There was great competition in the matter of decorations and lanterns. The doorway of every house was draped with embroideries, bead-curtains and multi-coloured lamps' (Gernet, 1962:188).

Bredon and Mitrophanow (1966: 137), writing of the nineteenth century, describe a street leading to Beijing's old Drum Tower that had 'until a few years ago, a special display of lanterns carved from blocks of ice, trimmed with cypress branches and decorated inside with bright paper figures of men and mountains'. Modern-day Harbin, in northern China's Heilongjiang province, still continues the tradition of carved ice lanterns during its world-famous annual Ice and Snow Festival.

Imperial Beijing's lantern market (*dengshikou*), a short walk from the Forbidden City, used to draw thousands of spectators, but the decline of the festival in the years after 1919 put the old workshops out of business. Ironically, the district has adapted in pace to the demands of modernity: today, it is the city's electrical fittings centre.

Once upon a time, creative lantern riddles (*dengmi*) or poems were pasted on the lanterns to amuse the more cultured and literary members of society. Unfortunately, the custom of original, hand-written poems has virtually died out. The Lantern Festival was also a time when those who had acquired fame or money were to 'offer their thanks to the deities... and people over 50 have each to hang a lantern at the Buddhist or ancestral temples as a sign of gratitude for their long life' (*Chinese Festivals*, 1976: 4).

Households that had seen the birth of a son during the year were expected to hang the largest and brightest lanterns (in Chinese, the rebus of *diandeng*, 'lighting a lantern', resembles *dianding*, 'adding a son'). In rural China and Hong Kong's New Territories, this observance is still respected.

Theatrical Performances and Dances

Theatrical performances, special dances, and acrobatics that include stilt-walking have long been popular during the Lantern Festival. Attended by great throngs of crowds, themselves catered to by endless streams of noisy street merchants and hawkers, the most fashionable today are the *shehuo*, unique performances combining theatre, song, dance, and acrobatic stunts. Each Chinese community seems to have its own variation in an almost unlimited spectrum, but one of the most popular sees the dressing of very young children in traditional costumes. The children are carried through the streets on small, high platforms, often several levels tall, with two- and three-year-olds poised above a tier of five-year olds. Some sources believe that these *shehuo* performances evolved from the ancient costumed exorcism rites held on the twenty-fourth day of the previous lunar month to ward off evil spirits (see Chapter 2).

Also popular at this time of year are popular rural folk dances known as *yangko*, performed to traditional *yangge* (literally, 'rice-sprouting songs'). These folk dances are now sometimes combined with stilt-walking to form a unique and amusing, decidedly more circus-like, diversion.

The dragon dance, performed by a long chain of men who carry a 7- to 10-metre cloth- or paper-covered bamboo frame depicting a gold, green, or red dragon, is today almost exclusively reserved for display during the Lantern Festival. Consisting of as few as nine or as many as twenty-four sections, the dragon traditionally chases a white pearl carried by a member of the performance troupe. The largest dragon dance in the world today is held in San Francisco as the highlight of the annual Chinese-American Golden Dragon Parade.

Multicultural Singapore has successfully combined the traditional Chinese *shehuo* performances with local and international entertainment troupes to create a popular parade held on a weekend evening following the Lunar New Year. Known as the Chingay Parade, it attracts hundreds of thousands of spectators.

Folk-tales and Traditional Foods

A number of Chinese folk-tales are associated with the fifteenth day of the first lunar month. History records the day as that chosen by Wendi (r. 179–157 BC), the popular third emperor of the Northern Zhou dynasty, for his coronation. Although a son of Gaozu, the dynasty's founder, Wendi did not reign but for the intervention of a loyal general named Zhou Bo, who suppressed an attempt to usurp the throne that was led in part by one of Gaozu's wives, the infamous Empress Lü.

A popular food consumed during the Lantern Festival is called *yuanxiao* (literally, 'first full moon', its shape certainly resembling a full moon), a stuffed, glutinous rice flour ball which is eaten in a 'first soup' (*tangyuan*). *Yuanxiao* can be stuffed with a variety of pastes and fillings ranging from sweet black bean paste to shredded pork. Generally, meat fillings are more popular in the Cantonese-speaking south, sweet-paste fillings in the Mandarin-speaking north. Tianjin is known for its *yuanxiao* stuffed with honey and white grapes, Zhejiang for those filled with crab meat.

The bacchanal nature of this ancient holiday, which lasted as long as five days during the Song dynasty (AD 960–1279), has faded in the modern Chinese world, and today it is celebrated more sedately and modestly, although no less joyfully.

6

The Diversity of Chinese New Year Traditions

THE BASIC ELEMENTS of the Chinese New Year are not alien to any Chinese community, but some add practices or observations that further enrich the special holiday through their own unique cultural associations. Described here are a few of the more common variations on the holiday from throughout the Chinese world.

Mainland China: The Spring Festival

Officially, the Lunar New Year, which is based on the lunar calendar and so is one of society's 'olds', is no longer recognized in mainland China. It is the welcoming of spring and the Spring Festival that the mainland celebrates, and the celebration is no less colourful, exciting, extravagant, and tradition-rich as that of any Lunar New Year. An added benefit is the private enjoyment by the populace of fire-crackers and fireworks, except where they are banned, although the ban is largely ignored in many parts of the country.

As in most societies, it is in the rural areas that the traditional practices receive the most careful attention. In addition, many towns and regional centres have their own indigenous holiday practices. In Shaoxing, Zhejiang province, for example, an important part of the Spring Festival is attendance at operas and plays honouring a local village deity. Observing their own traditions, many of China's ethnic minorities also celebrate the arrival of the new year at about this time of the year. Among the minority groups there is a diversity of New Year practices and observations—ranging from the Dong people's bullfight to the blackening of faces by the Daur people—the exploration of which goes far beyond the scope of this small handbook.

Hong Kong

In many ways, Hong Kong is one of the most traditional and hence 'standard' celebrants of the Chinese Lunar New Year. A main deviation from the dominant form is Hong Kong's downplaying of the Lantern Festival on the fifteenth day of the first moon—perhaps because Hong Kong culture is largely southern Chinese (predominantly flavoured by Guangdong influences) and the traditional Lantern Festival has always been a more northern celebration. In Hong Kong the pageantry associated with the Lantern Festival has been moved to other dates. The 'real' Lantern Festival takes place at the time of the Mid-Autumn Festival, on the fifteenth day of the eighth month, when all of Hong Kong spills out into the Territory's parks, carrying bright lanterns to celebrate the holiday.

A procession of costumed children balanced on elevated poles and platforms, commonly a part of the Lantern Festival's *shehuo* performances, is witnessed in Hong Kong on the island of Cheung Chau during the famous Cheung Chau Bun Festival, held late in the spring. Lion dances can be seen during the Cheung Chau festival, as well as at Chinese New Year and on the island of Kau Sai, near Sai Kung, during its annual Hung Shing Festival, observed on the thirteenth day of the second lunar month.

What truly sets Hong Kong apart from Asia's other Chinese cities during the Lunar New Year celebrations are the spectacular neon decorations installed on many of the Territory's commercial buildings. While retailers throughout the region decorate for the back-to-back festive seasons of Christmas and Chinese New Year, no other city matches Hong Kong in its array. A popular custom at this time of year is an evening stroll beside the harbour to enjoy the vivid display (Plate 18).

Straits Chinese and Hokkiens

Sugar cane has long been central to the economy and culture of the Straits Chinese, and its inclusion in New Year's observances exemplifies its importance. According to tradition, during the Song dynasty a group of Hokkiens escaped massacre by imperial troops led by the evil General Yang Lu-lang by hiding amongst the tall stalks in a field of sugar cane. The massacre is said to have ended on the eve of the ninth day of the New Year (the day celebrated as the birthday of the Jade Emperor), and sugar cane remains an essential component of Straits Chinese altars on this day.

Other scholars believe only that sugar cane represents a long and sweet life to the Straits Chinese, who were among the first to promote its cultivation on the Malaysian peninsula. Whatever the origin of the practice, in traditional households freshly cut sugar cane is put behind each door to ward off evil on New Year's Eve, and one still sees a pair of freshly cut stalks tied to the trunk of a Straits Chinese bridal car to ensure that the newlyweds enjoy a 'sweet' life together.

Other Straits Chinese variants on the celebration of Chinese New Year are primarily culinary and linguistic. In the Malay spoken by the Baba, for example, the standard New Year's greeting is *Mintak huntong, huntong panjang, panjang, panjang umor* ('Wishing you every good luck and a long life')(Cheo and Speeden, 1988: 55).

On the second day of the New Year, men of the Straits Chinese community visit their families' ancestral graves (some regions in mainland China, in Gansu province for example, also follow this practice). On the last day of the New Year (the fifteenth day of the first month), special dishes called *nasi pulot* and *pengat* are made and offered to the ancestors in the morning hours. These dishes are made from a variety of sweets and symbolize the good luck and blessings of the season.

To the usual array of auspicious dishes the Straits Chinese add the banana, whose colour is reminiscent of gold, sticky glutinous rice, representing riches and togetherness, and *sireh kaya*, a golden yellow sweet coconut custard.

Indonesia

Chinese New Year celebrations are kept low-key in Indonesia due to the historic hostilities between ethnic Chinese and the Muslim majority. Chinese Indonesians are officially 'reminded' each year to keep their Lunar New Year celebrations within the confines of the law, as officially expressed in the 1967 *Presidential Instructions on Religion, Beliefs, and Chinese Customs and Practices*.

As a result, the public display of banners, pennants, printed material, ornaments, and symbols in celebration of the Chinese New Year are forbidden. In addition, the presentation at local Buddhist temples of public celebrations, dramas, dances, and events which have themes reflecting Chinese culture are also formally frowned upon. In general, celebrations are to be kept low-key and within the confines of the four walls of one's home—precepts which are not always kept to by the well-to-do Indonesian Chinese mercantile community.

Japan

Sadly, Japan's shrinking Chinese communities seldom celebrate the traditional Lunar New Year in the old style. As each generation became more and more acclimated to the Japanese way of life, the Lunar New Year gave way to the Western (and Japanese) practice of recognizing 1 January (in Japanese, Gantan) as the beginning of the new year. Chinese New Year is celebrated most commonly, if at all, with a special family dinner.

A few notable exceptions remain within Japan's three major Chinese communities in Yokohama, Kobe, and Nagasaki. East of Kannai, Yokohama's business centre, and next door to Yokohama Stadium, in the city's Chinatown, one or two small events are still arranged to celebrate the Lunar New Year. Kobe's Chinatown, along Nankin-machi, is home to a general Spring Festival held approximately one week after New Year's Day, and in Nagasaki, home of the country's oldest Chinese community, a city-wide mid-winter Lantern Festival is held, although its roots have long since been forgotten.

A Final Note

One thing became abundantly clear in researching this volume: no two Chinese families share precisely the same New Year traditions. Countless 'definitive' descriptions of this colourful holiday were found or recounted to the author, many in delightful contrast with one another. This is not strange given a culture that stretches from Beijing to Singapore and even beyond to all the other continents of the globe. Chinese tradition is ultimately flexible and allows an infinite variety of expressions. The basic rudiments of the holiday, although not necessarily their chronological order, in most cases remain unchanged, and the richness of their expression only serves to showcase the very richness and diversity of Chinese culture itself.

Notes

1. Different cultures have resolved this conflict in different ways. The Christian world, for example, adds a twenty-ninth day to the month of February once every four years. Islam follows a strictly lunar calendar and adds a full year at regular intervals.
2. Each of these twelve animals is in turn associated with a direction, a colour, an element, a time, and a planet. Chinese fortune-telling is based on such details of one's birth and is a fascinating subject in itself, but it is too extensive a topic to be covered here. Interested readers are referred to the Selected Bibliography.
3. *La* refers to a sacrifice, *ba* means 'eight', and *zhou* refers to 'gruel' or 'porridge'.
4. Traditionally *labazhou* is made from a combination of five grains— five being an auspicious number—such as millet, maize, sorghum, rice, and barley. Red dates are the most important fruit to be included. A variety of nuts and seeds is added towards the end of preparation, and sometimes brown sugar is added to sweeten the mixture.

    In Hong Kong this traditional broth has degenerated into a radish soup, probably because when 'the Cantonese adopted Chinese customs under the [Tang] Dynasty, the La Pa, or sacrifice of the eighth day, was corrupted into Lo Po or radish, and Radish Pudding it remains to this day' (Burkhardt, 1953: 67).
5. Tun Li-Ch'en (1987) writes that the eating of *labazhou* is one of the three Buddhist customs still surviving in China that probably has pre-Buddhist origins.
6. A northern Chinese tradition dictates that pancakes should be made on the twenty-third day of the last month, the house cleaned on the twenty-fourth, bean curd made on the twenty-fifth, pigs and sheep slaughtered on the twenty-sixth, chickens and ducks prepared on the twenty-seventh, dough for steamed buns made on the twenty-eighth, liquor bought on the twenty-ninth, and dumplings cooked on the thirtieth.
7. The term *Peranakan* is derived from the Malay word *anak*, 'child', and means 'local' or 'native-born'. The etymology of the term *Baba* is much debated, but it is also found in India, where it is an honorific used for males. Given the concurrence of the arrival of Indians and Chinese on the Malaysian subcontinent, the term may be Indian in origin. A Straits Chinese male is referred to as a *Baba*, a female as a *Nonya*, a term some scholars have linked to the Portuguese for 'grandmother'.

8. See Bodde (1975: 81ff) for a detailed discussion of the original festivals that contribute to the contemporary observances of Chinese New Year.

9. Although one source claims the timing in accordance with a 'social scale: ...by bureaucrats on the 23rd day... by laymen on the 24th and boat people on the 25th' (*Chinese Festivals*, 1976: 38).

10. Also known as Zaoshen, Zaojunshen, and Zaojun.

11. Cheo and Speeden (1988: 51) report that members of the Baba community of Malaysia did not follow the usual practice of smearing sweet things on the Kitchen God's lips, but 'merely offer[ed] the usual fruits and cakes, and burn[ed] the necessary joss paper to send off this hearth deity'.

12. Berkowitz and Brandauer (1969) report that 'the worship of the Kitchen God by the resettled villagers in Tai Po [a recently established town in Hong Kong's New Territories] has practically died out' as a result of lack of a suitable place to hang his portrait.

13. Two other women are often portrayed in Chinese art holding peaches of immortality. One is the beautiful goddess Magu, easily identified by her long fingernails; the other is He Xiangu, the sole female member of the group known as the Eight Daoist Immortals (*see* n. 18). The God of Longevity, Lao Shouxing, is also commonly depicted carrying an oversized peach. He is so frequently portrayed that few will be unfamiliar with his vast, protruding forehead, big ears, long drooping eyebrows, and rounded, robe-clad form.

14. Li (1956: 43–4, 49) notes that the Japanese apricot (*Prunus mume*) is Chinese in origin, where it is known as *mei*. 'In non-botanical literature, it is generally referred to as the "Plum" although botanically it does not belong to the Plum group but instead to the Apricot group.'

15. Red is the ultimate Chinese symbol of joy and is used in connection with all celebrations and special occasions. It is believed to have magical powers against evil. For these reasons, brides still wear red in China, and bridal processions were once marked by a red umbrella. Red cords were also used to unite the bride and groom's wine cups. In imperial times, the emperor signed his royal edicts in red ink. Yellow is a spiritual colour; in Chinese opera, for example, yellow faces identify the gods. It is also the colour used for spring couplets that are hung in temples.

16. On a more sophisticated linguistic level, the picture of a bat plus the character meaning longevity together with two coins expresses a benediction for 'double happiness'. The riddle is solved as follows: *fu* means both 'bat' and 'happiness'; *shou* is the character meaning 'longevity', and the two coins are a homophone for 'double happi-

ness', as *shuang* means 'two' or 'a pair' and *qian*, meaning 'money', does double duty for *quan* ('complete'). This rebus was solved from a small vase in the Musée Guimet in Paris that is decorated by both the picture as well as the double-meaning text. It is one of the 'Rosetta stones' of understanding Chinese symbolic art.

17. A pond full of fish or a painting of a school of fish represents a wish for success and wealth. A village pond teeming with fish is a common subject in the newly popular 'primitive' school of Chinese art.

18. The Eight Daoist Immortals are a group of eight quasi-historical figures said to have abandoned the civilized world, retreating to live in harmony with nature, practising spiritual and mental discipline and shunning cooked food to live on pine cones and dew in order to attain immortality.

19. This *he* is pronounced with a soft 'e' as in 'her'.

20. In some rural areas wells are still decorated with red paper charms at Chinese New Year to mark their importance and to protect them for the year to come.

21. A popular Cantonese New Year snack is *chin duy*, made of mixed peanuts, sesame seeds, popcorn, and molasses rolled into balls or flat discs and then fried.

22. Each city has its own preferred fortune-telling temples, but Hong Kong's Wong Tai Sin temple, in Kowloon, overshadows all others in reputation and popularity.

23. Ng quotes a neighbour who claims that the red packets were used to pass extortion money from the businesses to triads, the local organized crime organizations. Each 'lucky envelope' was said to contain no less than A$500.

24. Bredon and Mitrophanow, 1966: 125ff. Tun Li-Ch'en (1987), writing of the same superstitions, notes only the first eight days.

25. In pinyin Chaozhou, but also seen as Tiuchew. Teochow is the most commonly found transliteration of the name and dialect of this important Chinese community from the Chaozhou district of eastern Guangdong province. The dialect most resembles a combination of Cantonese and the southern Min dialect.

26. Actual ingredients can include fresh, candied, and pickled melon, red and white sour ginger, candied lime, pomelo, sweet potato, carrots, white radish, leek, cucumber, wax gourd, ground peanuts, sesame seeds, jellyfish, and a biscuit resembling gold pieces, all in addition to the fish (which may be such delicacies as swordfish, salmon, grouper, lobster, or abalone).

The Chinese Zodiac

Rat
1924, 1936, 1948, 1960, 1972, 1984, 1996

Ox
1925, 1937, 1949, 1961, 1973, 1985, 1997

Tiger
1926, 1938, 1950, 1962, 1974, 1986, 1998

Rabbit
1927, 1939, 1951, 1963, 1975, 1987, 1999

Dragon
1928, 1940, 1952, 1964, 1976, 1988, 2000

Snake
1929, 1941, 1953, 1965, 1977, 1989, 2001

Horse
1930, 1942, 1954, 1966, 1978, 1990, 2002

Sheep
1931, 1943, 1955, 1967, 1979, 1991, 2003

Monkey
1932, 1944, 1956, 1968, 1980, 1992, 2004

Rooster
1933, 1945, 1957, 1969, 1981, 1993, 2005

Dog
1934, 1946, 1958, 1970, 1982, 1994, 2006

Pig
1935, 1947, 1959, 1971, 1983, 1995, 2007

Selected Bibliography

A Year of Good Fortune: Legends of the Rooster and Traditions of the Chinese New Year (1993), guidebook of an exhibition, China Institute in America, 19 January to 6 March, New York: China Institute in America.

Alexeiev, Basil M. (1983), *The Chinese Gods of Wealth: A Lecture*, Singapore: Cybille Orient Gallery Pte Ltd.

Baker, Hugh (1979), *Ancestral Images: A Hong Kong Album*, Hong Kong: South China Morning Post Ltd.

Berkowitz, Morris, and Brandauer, Frederick P. (1969), *Folk Religion in an Urban Setting: A Study of Hakka Villagers in Transition*, Hong Kong: Christian Study Centre on Chinese Religion and Culture.

Bodde, Derk (1975), *Festivals in Classical China: New Year and other Annual Observances during the Han Dynasty 206 BC–AD 220*, Princeton: Princeton University Press.

Bredon, Juliet, and Mitrophanow, Igor (1966), *The Moon Year: A Record of Chinese Customs and Festivals* (reprint of the original 1927 edition published in Shanghai), New York: Paragon Book Reprint Corp.

Burkhardt, V. R. (1953), *Chinese Creeds & Customs*, Hong Kong: South China Morning Post Ltd.

Chavannes, Edouard (1973), *The Five Happinesses: Symbolism in Chinese Popular Art* (translated, annotated, and illustrated by Elaine Spaulding Atwood), New York: Weatherhill.

Chen Jingwen (1996), 'Ushering in wealth and good luck,' *The Sunday Times* (Singapore), 4 February, p. 3.

Cheng Hou-tien (1976), *The Chinese New Year*, New York: Holt, Rinehart and Winston.

Cheo Kim Ban, and Speeden, Muriel (1988), *Baba Folk Beliefs and Superstitions*, Singapore: Landmark Books Pte Ltd.

Chinese Festivals (1976), Hong Kong: The Chartered Bank.

Crow, Carl (1938), *The Chinese Are Like That*, New York: Harper and Brothers.

Dennys, Nicholas B. (1968), *The Folklore of China* (reprint of the original 1876 edition published in Hong Kong), Amsterdam: Oriental Press.

Eberhard, Wolfram (1952), *Chinese Festivals*, New York: Schumm.

— (1986), *Dictionary of Chinese Symbols* (translated by G. L. Campbell), London: Routledge and Kegan Paul, 1986.

Gernet, Jacques (1962), *Daily Life in China: On the Eve of the Mongol Invasion 1250–1276* (translated by H. M. Wright), New York: Macmillan.

Hong Kong China Tourism Press (1993), *The Grand Spectacle of Chinese New Year Customs*, Hong Kong: Hong Kong China Tourism Press.

Jenyns, Soame (1966), *A Background to Chinese Painting*, New York: Schocken Books.

John, Alan Robert (1991), 'Reunion', in Leon Comber, ed., *Prizewinning Asian Fiction*, Hong Kong: Hong Kong University Press, pp. 43–50.

Kong, Shiu L. (1989), *Chinese Culture and Lore*, Hong Kong: University of Toronto Press.

Lee Siow Mong (1986), *Spectrum of Chinese Culture*, Malaysia: Pelanduk Publications (M) Sdn Bhd.

Li, H. L. (1956), *Chinese Flower Arrangement*, Philadelphia: Hedera House.

Ng, Lillian (1994), *Silver Sister*, Melbourne: Mandarin Australia.

Ng, Rebecca S. Y., and Ingram, Shirley C. (1983), *Chinese Culture in Hong Kong*, Hong Kong: n.p.

Ong Hean-Tatt (1993), *Chinese Animal Symbolism*, Malaysia: Pelanduk Publications (M) Sdn Bhd.

Singapore Clan Foundation (1989), *Chinese Customs and Festivals in Singapore*, Singapore: Landmark Books Pte Ltd.

Smith, Arthur H. (1965), *Proverbs and Common Sayings from the Chinese*, New York: Dover Publications Inc. (reprint of the 1914 original published in Shanghai by the American Presbyterian Mission Press).

Stepanchuk, Carol, and Wong, Charles (1991), *Mooncakes and Hungry Ghosts: Festivals of China*, Hong Kong: China Books.

Tun Li-Ch'en (1987), included in Derk Bodde, trans., *Annual Customs and Festivals in Peking* (original publication data unknown), Hong Kong: Hong Kong University Press.

Vaughan, J. D. (1971), *The Manners and Customs of the Chinese* (a reprint of the 1879 original published by the Mission Press, Singapore, as *The Manners and Customs of the Chinese of the Straits Settlements*), Singapore: Oxford University Press.

Wang Shucun (1996), 'Chinese Folk Art: An Interview with Wang Shucun', *Orientations*, 27(1)(January): 53–5.

Ward, Barbara E., and Law, Joan (1995), *Chinese Festivals in Hong Kong*, Hong Kong: The Guidebook Company Ltd.

Index